THE WEIGHT
OF
DROUGHT

THE WEIGHT OF DROUGHT

Tyler Michael Jacobs

STEPHEN F. AUSTIN STATE UNIVERSITY PRESS

Permissions
Stephen F. Austin State University Press
P.O. Box 13007, SFA Station
Nacogdoches, TX 75962
sfapress@sfasu.edu
936.468.1078

ISBN: 978-1-62288-286-1

Production Manager: Kimberly Verhines
Cover Design: Paris Taylor
Book Design: Tolina Rowlands

Also by Tyler Michael Jacobs

Building Brownville

For Lila and Jasper

CONTENTS

TWO

ACKNOWLEDGMENTS

Thanks to the editors of the following journals and programs in which some of these poems first appeared, sometimes in different form: *Anti-Heroin Chic, Kissing Dynamite,* Nebraska Public Media's *Friday LIVE, The Oakland Arts Review, Passages North, Pidgeonholes, Plainsongs, Sierra Nevada Review,* and *Variant Literature.*

"Thoughts on Exiting a Building" was featured in conjunction with the Them Myself & Us exhibition during ArtsX at Bowling Green State University.

ONE

STILL LIFE

I stretch my arms out toward the empty
Pasture I keep returning to where the paw
Of hoof striking soil and the piss
Striking soil and the ripping of ryegrass
By rippling bodies once filled this grazing.
The thunder that filled my reaching no longer
Opens out across the worn-down ryegrass.
The trees have since winnowed their leaves
And February rain falls right through them
Striking soil. Remember the moonlight
And the ryegrass and the rabbits in the ryegrass
And the scars of moonlight striking soil? I do.
I can't tell if what I reach toward reaches back
But everything is reaching. When I tell you
I miss horses, I'm saying I miss something to hold.

SUMMER HOUSE

The walls were up all night sweating.
Warm breeze holds a bare chest in moon-

Scar. As if out of sorrow, this house seems
To breathe. Curtains billow inward

Wanting to drape us in voile. A different kind
Of poise. The walls want to press

Against floor's pockmarked face to cool themselves
Of this raw heat. Did I only dream of cricket

Sound beckoning me toward birth? Rattling
Its many fingers, the house fan floats in

Morning dew and velvet birdsong. Eventually
Rain cloud rags sky. The windows must be closed.

The curtains as calming beams
Of elegance. The rough grip of weather-

Worn timber callouses. The house wood aches
Through rooms to bend any listening ear.

THE WEIGHT OF DROUGHT

A life without trees saddens me.

When a cloud drifts off
Into land, it's saying goodbye.

Your house, just a house when I'm able to imagine a life
I can live without you.

Somewhere I once was
A body.

My body:
Blessings caught
In teeth. Sliver-
Words in morning light.

There was just enough blushing
To call it joy.

No one can hold you the way the earth does.

It took me a lifetime to learn
That kind of holding is a form of begging.

A cloud exhales into tomorrow.

Look,
I watch light quiver the street
Before it begins spitting.

You extend one hand, wherever you are, expecting to catch rain.

THERE ARE SO MANY OTHER STORIES
TO TELL

When you complained about the onset of cold and the gravestones
   kept singing
The virginity of the dead, both must be the same thing.

My feet still try to find yours in the middle of the night to fall
Back to sleep. Fingers once braided together as if to say, I'm here,

Blossoming rosebuds in palms. It's that cold emptiness
Of morning in which I wake. A moth tapping the screen

And the smell of the last of autumn through the open window
In my apartment. I look at my feet wanting something warm to
   press

Them against. I'm tired of this awful color.
The treetops are sweeping the sky today. It's that line

Between birth and dying. O, trees in stale light, forgive me
For not noticing it's the shadows that move and with nowhere
   to rest a head.

ON BEING DIRT

In turn, each bell quakes, sifts air as if to draw clear lines
Where the wind sits and where we begin. All a whisper
Into my sorrowing. I think now of the time you exhaled
A river into me.

*

There is a flower, I said. Pluck it from me
Like a rib. The plants along this path are older than the stars
We held up our phones to see. I told you I can't see the color
Of a rainbow.

*

The way you described it to me wasn't enough:
In pockmark sky, an envelope of glitter taken hold of
By wind, a screaming of blossom into horizon where sun-drunk
Pilgrims drift into what looks like shore.

*

Then you stopped.

Much like the bird reaching upward with a partially opened mouth,

We searched for sustenance. The moon lurched forward into the
    hard

Break of relief when the heart settled into hesitant spark. I hear

The sounding of bells again.

*

Through cover of raincloud,

Everything is enough. Now, look at the empty glass in my hand,

Think of the fleeting seasons that fall across my cheek.

OUTSIDE THE GARDEN

This sky's life in the water and the water in the soil and the sky and
    the soil
In the water tastes every history that ever had been and never was
    in the water,
In the water swooning into itself and the water that doesn't.
Histories and histories of blood and bile in the water and in the
    water
In the field flooding and in the roads washed out in the water,
In the water cutting its teeth on spit.
Water filling the dying cow's mouth with the sky and the water in
    the cow
Washes the cow to ornate its tongue with cleanliness in the water,
In the water resisting and the water resisting.
Skin and teeth on the soil and in the water in the soil and the
    erosion of the soil
In the water cleaning the wound with the sky and the soil in the
    water,
In the water revealing dead body after dead body after dead body.
This soil is swollen with the water in it and the sky in this water
And the only way to touch this sky is to touch the reflection of it in
    the water,
In the water opening its mother-face.

FORGIVE ME

A dilated pupil carries the same weight
The sky holds up from crashing

Into us. Even the light we see doesn't stop
There, echoing multitudes of never ending

Pasts. When a star explodes, a lifetime,
We imagine, forms in the eye if it wasn't already

Alive, and breathing like universes still
As grains of sand. What we found didn't last.

SAGE GREEN HOUSE

I once ate my evenings
Of burnt button

Mushrooms. So much time to want
Nothing more than pots

Of flowers, or a garden of them,
To plant and look at.

I once admired this green house
Down the street and would dip

A brush into green paint
And run the bristles along siding.

After I would finish,
I'd take a step back to examine

My hard work
And wipe the sweat from my brow.

ADORNING THE TABLE:

The peach and the flower both indulge this table:
Each a different kind of hunger:
One carries the life in which you exist:
The other carries the life in which you don't:
Every table you've ever sat at has held something:
Like obsession, I sit opposite you:
Sometimes it's the table we set:
Sometimes it's not the table we wish we had:
Like this one on which these flowers keep:
Or this one on which these peaches keep:
Here, obsession lies in the centerpiece:
Each head turned slightly toward the eye:
Brushed with light and—now:
What was it I was saying about hunger?

FIRST SNOW, UNDER THE CARILLON

You point out the large round cap of a mushroom
Buried under autumnal leaves
That seems to keep itself alive with the persistent

Leaves I keep sifting through to uncover the fruiting
Body that I know, too, won't survive:
I, too, have come to love entire ecosystems.

We huddle from the cold and watch
How the snow heavies the air—I want to say me
But it's the moment that falls—

As quiet as I remember any November being
Except for the bells,
Sad, sad, sad. Yes, I'm singing.

FORAGED ACORNS

Winter glimmers out of night's belly
To flourish into prairie sky.

Only the wind sings from the shiver
Of branches off which wisps of snow plume

Into flat, mutable light. I watch as it drapes
Over the croquis on my desk

Which still feels like too much commitment.
I wait for the iron water to sadden the color

Of yarn now cooling in the pot on my stove.
The yarn falls into the shape of my hand

As if it has already learned to embrace
The body's desire. I inspect it, hang it to dry.

THIS, TOO, WAS REAL. I PROMISE.

We hear the distance sundering.
I wanted to tell you: *I'm trying to feel*
This, too. Here, where the fire was,
I could feel what the fire made:
How many lives we had to live
To get to this one. I walked over
And walked over: A field wanting,
Sprouting like a field again. I knew this
Then when the clouds became storm
Clouds. And there you were leading
Me to a horse refusing the bit,
Or to a horse with a bit-full mouth.
Either way, a horse sounding like a horse,
The dry, soft dirt getting wetter.

AUBADE

Each bellied cloud, swelling with give, pouring over horizon,

Becomes night, becomes morning, becomes daylight, becomes
ordinary auspices

In the same way I see this life surprising if it surprises.

SHARING AN APPLE

Evening lights us through the meadow of empty
Deer beds nodding with tallgrass, white wood aster,
And mayapple. A deer lies down to chew
On cud, or, perhaps, to hide itself from you, me, or the wind.
The warmth starts to chill as shadows lengthen
But I find myself sitting in tree root watching
The leaves pierce delicate air
And blemish the pond's murky face.
I watch a damselfly plunge its copper-tinged abdomen
Into the water, how little moments make a life—
I watch as you toss the apple core into the woods
As if away means gone and think
How one act can hold so much weight. The air
Thickens deep in the old-growth forest where wind disappears
Into every thirsting thing:
Moss claims every fallen snag,
Every sawed-off tree stump reminds us
To be tender with ourselves, to feel the dirt
In our shivered palms, to remain idle
For a moment longer.
The grazing fawn watches us the same as we watch her.

EVEN GOD MUST SEARCH FOR MEANING

        watching the moonstruck dead
And what December has done
To the body's dark eaves.
If ever they were blossomless,
How vivid the dead burden
With grief-sounds
Only their bodies make heard.
The sound of the distance
Is the sound of that bellowing:
The body carries
The body's pain—
                      Is it the soul
That utters the light
Into plumes? Acceptance is
A form of allowance
                   Swelling
With snow that never falls.
The sky covets what it can't
Hold, then waits. How can I not look up
And see a surface,
A history of familiar things?

THE FIRST FRUIT SPEAKS ON BEING EATEN

The throat is an awful room
Because that's what I've been
Taught. I keep knowing my garden
As a body, because that will make it seen,
Touched. What was never bitten is
Always clean and I wanted to be eaten:
Envious little notes of dirt-
Stained rot, wine-dark bruises—
Fruiting shadows that constellate my flesh,
Now. I watched, because I was shown,
The culling of any breathing thing;
Mouths of eternal emptiness.
Through creeping bentgrass, horsetail,
And nutsedge,
The wind blew in a childishness;
All that sky and no water.
The cruel face of God.

ORDAINED THE SELF BODY

Summer heat makes the mind
An antique candle.

I felt myself softening
The way a sapling aches

Into centuries of grief, having realized
A man who becomes a reflection

Becomes a statue of thorn:
An angle

Washed out of
A clean only hunger knows,

Begging the moon to forgive him
For hating the moon-shaped

Scar on his throat.
My body is just body.

I watch water blanket prairie
Into perfumed air.

THE ART OF HATCHING

The mother's hatchlings
Will die
If they become hatchlings

At all. How could he
Have known?
The child—

Just wanting to be
That color, carrying lament
In his palm,

Bears the burden
Of a life—still
Doesn't know

What it is
To die, dropped
The egg and watched it bloom.

YOU'RE NOT SEEING THE MOUNTAIN

Look how beautiful the flowers are before they wound:
Their tongues mouthing everything
Until each finds itself against a cheek.
Everything held eventually dies.

Everything held eventually dies
Like this bouquet against your cheek
Which the petals have been licking since
I wanted you to look at the fucking flowers.

NEBRASKA

It was the rural over which I watched
Folds of light shake themselves
Across the landscape.
On either side of me is a field
Waiting to be worked or planted.
I know this as prayer—
Pray for rain then pray
For any yield at all. This landscape forgets
The lifetime of dust-ridden springs
And callused hands that tell me:
Yes, we were here. Yes, we feared
The dryness. Yes, we know it might
Last one more night. Yes, if it lasts
One more night, we're dead.
Rain will eventually unburden the sky
Because we believe it will. This life is
A mirror with nothing left to say.

HATCHLINGS

The mother perches
Next to her fallen and empty nest.
On the ground, fluid spills
From the broken shells:
Translucent, unformed
Bodies scatter onto the lawn.
A heaviness overtakes the wind,
Today. Her grief-sounds trill
As any mother's would.

ON GOD

Wind ruins everything, like it does, by spitting sand in your eye.

CARRION, OR SOMETHING LIKE IT

Think about the rotting carcass in the sun:
Think of its eyes: cut from the sockets;
Think of its ears: ripped from the head;
Think of its tongue and its lips:
How they're both cut from the mouth;
Think about the broken jaw
And the pulled-out teeth; think about both
Halves of the body: each once occupied
The same space; think of its genitals:
Mutilated in the groin; think of its anus:
Eaten or cut from the body;
Think about how the blood swans on the ground.

TWO

THE HORSE ENTERS A LIFE THE SAME WAY
BREATH LEAVES THE BODY

Today, she gallops toward me, nostrils huffing, and eats
The oats from my palm until the oats are gone
And my hand drips with saliva. I trace her years
Through vertebrae, down one rippling
Leg to a filthy hoof and then another
To pick the hurt and what she can't from her soles.
The horse enters a life the same way breath leaves the body.
She snorts in my hair. Her sorrel coat stains
My hand with dust; carries drought
Through a field; tail swats hunger
From her back; teeth gnaw fence posts to fill
Herself with more than thirst.
The horse enters a life the same way breath leaves the body
And I want to know if breaking is
The burden we carry or the price
She pays to live on this earth
Tomorrow.   While she eats the apple
I feed her, her black and bottomless eyes
Recognize me the same way
She set her last hoof down as if pleased.
My fingers nudge her muzzle and she turns,
Bucking into silhouette.

IN FULL BLOSSOM

The rosette of a musk thistle submits
Itself toward the earth. As I look
At my pierced and swollen,
Dust-caked hand, I fear
I've never known love.
My dead father plants pines
In a field I once ran through out of
Love or some other mysterious thing.
Do I make this memory of cloth spit
Or bird nest or cloud street
As if bearing pain
Might make of itself a festival of years?
The Nebraska conehead pierces tonight's
Room. I wish you could hear them as I do.

MY FATHER'S HAND WAS A SHOVEL

Many nights I wake from dreams
About the lifeless body of a dog—
Elbow deep from digging
Because my father handed me the spade.
When I finish, my father kneels
And takes my cheek in his palm:

Oh, Tyler, I envy any day it doesn't take grief
For you to feel like you've become a man.
And I feel the dirt underneath my fingernails.
And he takes my fist in his hands
And I feel my hand opening
In my father's—only then
Do I know we are different men.

My mistake was looking for too long
At the way the light washed the dog's eyes,
I believed they lustered with me—

STILL LIFE

All these buildings
Stand with open
Mouths to taste

The orange
I peel thinking
Of the Ponderosa

Pines I'm gathered in.
All those
Needles,

Lost in name,
Bear the weight
Of still air. When

A pine is planted,
I forgive myself.
Now, I plant flowers

For no other reason
Than to sing.
I want that

Clove-like aroma
To fill me.
Did I grasp

For the throat
Of the lily
As though there were still time?

STILL LIFE

Through the clearings of fallen
Timber, the sun

Empties itself
And I open up

To feel it completely.
I think of my father,

How every good man
Knows a rifle,

Why a tree splits like a head
To know happiness.

MORNING COFFEE

The silhouette of the dead fly
Against the backdrop of windowpane and blush

Of cold blue air dangles in silk, perhaps
The knotted thread of a sweater brushing sky

As if waiting to be ripped from the hem
Of window frame. Like the fly in his own fragile

Waits to extend toward eventual,
A hand on the cheek gestures the body.

An act opposite appetite—it wasn't until later
That the spider, like the leaves curtailing

From trees outside the window, curled and brittle
On the floor in countless moments of silence,

Unlike the sky which closes into itself,
Took the dead blossom of it, ever narrowing.

WILDFIRES

Everything is burning
And one by one they jump—
The bodies of wild horses fill
The sky and they're burning,
Too. Then their bodies feel
As if they never stop
Falling. Ash—the horse.
God, horse. My father the horse.
And I've wrapped my arms
Around that powerful
Neck a thousand times
Over. Not out of fear,
Or for love, but because I could
Touch the burned horse's teeth
Through holes in the cheek,
Because the beaten
Horse never deserved
That kick to the gut, because
The horse needed nothing
More than to be close
To something so I let myself
Be close to him
Like I'm a child again
Riding my mother's horse.
I loved that horse
Who broke bits and reins.
That horse gave me the feeling
Of falling that never left
Me. As I hit the parched
Soil after being thrown

From that muscled,
Bucking body, I broke
Into dust lifted by what felt
Like wind where I would later
Scatter his ashes between a shelter-
Belt of pine trees.
Where I would watch him
Plume into wind.
Then nothing special happened.
Then, sudden light, sudden heat:
My father's arms
A fire burning ever since.

PATCHWORK

Cut squares of fabric fall from the sewing
Desk as if the air wants clothed in grace, too.
Wisps of thread trail softly behind
Like smoldering embers after fire. The light
Shakes from the flickering bulb
Slipping across carpet into burnt-like folding
Mountains of chiffon, wool, linen, and gingham.
These fabric mountainsides have been burning
For years. The way it brightens this room
With its profound and violent peaks
Is the needle's harsh intrusions across the hem
Or collar which now hold a modest stitching.
When you wore it,
The seam fit clean across the shoulders
And pieced work fell over your ribs. How its days
Will end like when you fell into and out of love.
How it drank the scent of you which still remains
Long after you've gone: A different kind of fire.

SOMETIMES

When slat-light spills across shadowed
Walls, all these corners seem unfamiliar—

See how even the forgotten-about-flower
Arrived home to somehow

Seems indelible, perfect? The dead cling
Themselves onto themselves,

Fascinated by their own fascination.

STRUCTURES

I was taught how to love
The way cut stems drop

From the flowers onto countertops
And to the kitchen floor as if each were

Bones of winter and each blossoming
Were meant to be examined,

But only at a distance. I learned how
Words explode from my mouth

And that my lips kiss every time
I say, *please*; how they could cut

Like winter chills when I said,
Leave. I know the flattened bird on the street

Cannot nest toward morning,
That everyone sits with knees cleaved

Tight to their chest in the shower
And I learned how much weight it takes to fall.

I built a bridge out of toothpicks,
Assembling many small triangles first.

Gluing them together, I constructed
My Warren trusses.

Each triangle ached for something greater.

STILL LIFE

At some point
Even trees go
Silent. Under
Heavy sky
Swelling
With rain
And what I
Once found
Below it,
The chorus
Of grass
Scratching
Against itself
As it drowns
In air. A mother
Watches her calf
The way one
Describes lilies
Before she sniffs
And licks her new-
Born into breath
As if born
Once again
From the mouth
Like mineral-lick,
Salt-lick, the lick
Of a hand
By a calf
Abandoned
By its mother

Nudging toward
The bottle
I now hold
In my hands.
Had I asked
For this life,
Would I
Have it?
If not
For walking
Through it,
Then standing
And looking
On at what
I—if even
I wanted—
Could not
Create.

POEM

Not quite seen; yet, barren field still; something more tangible,
  please;

In harsh afternoon light, I notice the reflection of my eye in the
  lens of my glasses;

It's as if I can see my father again, for a moment, before the light is
  gone, as the dog eats the last of the cut banana from my palm.

INCANTATION

Maybe it isn't reach but the grasping at and the letting go of.
We drink from the faucet to keep alive. Here, like this,
And take turns sipping from our own palms.
If this is not a devotion, then show me what a devotion is.
Show me how the unsaddled horse shakes itself
Into sky's ancient windows, or how the sorrow
On a distant hill, when a tree dies, pries each clot-hold,
Or cloud-sigh, from those same windows.
The gesture of wind moves through
The leaves of the best trees and the best horses, kisses
Their rotting foreheads and names them mourning. Devotion
Shivers from my chest and blossoms mouth. But it carries
The weight of every drink: If you believe that weight, tell me
And I'll drink forever.

PASTORAL

If I were to believe
In nothing, devoured

By the body's
Unfurnished garden,

I would make of myself
An eternity: clouds

As beasts
Folding beast

In the mouth
Of the meadow,

And fruit so tart,
So divine that we eat

Tongue-sharp,
Blistered.

THE CHICKENS OF ST. CROIX

are feral. Much like what was made of you,
Agrestal land in want of sugar. As you heard

The waves, the water began to lick at you.
You hate what

You know: a home with a stone face
Where the wind doesn't even bother.

And that's when you leaned back into it,
Baptizing yourself in the Caribbean

To let go of who you are and to feel
Like the stars,

Or the horizon. The body welcomes that sway
Of the water. See how

You make yourself a map:
All pastoral-like and waiting to be read.

It only feels like you aren't yourself
Yet so you just watch the chickens

And, in that moment, the breeze swings
In and it is as if they took flight.

AFTER CLOUDS, THE TREES RAIN

Tornado sirens exhale over
The neighborhood in which I now live
Reminding us to feel the music
That spills from windows like the thrill
Of light on grass. I'm thinking
Of the divorced mother
Who teaches her son to dance,
To move his feet in tempo,
To hold up his palm and then wait—
He learns we hold on to compliments
The same way we hold on to the body
Of whom we love, clinging,
As if to stop the body from dying
Into itself. She understands loneliness
Passes like one hears the moment
Between a breath and an exhale—
Her hand rests in his palm
As each takes a deep breath.

THOUGHTS ON EXITING A BUILDING

The elms reflecting knuckled glares in glass

Braid into themselves. You don't want to let that fragility

On those trees break and fall into street's

Dark pavements.

All you can do is watch the leaves dry before they fall knowing

They can't shade you much longer.

Tell me what about today

Veiled every somber touch. Was it day

Stretching out onto the lawn of leaf's folded palms?

Or the long sun of evening quivering your masked body?

Your shadow on the wall?

It's quiet before these trees wisp into echo.

It's beautiful isn't it,

That looming?

LATE DAY SHADOWS

The light slips away, at first unnoticed,
In silent towns. The woman, throwing her purse
Over her shoulder, clutching it like a scowl,
Exits the Ford first. Then her husband. She enters
The grocery store. Bending in the wind,
And leaning against the passenger side fender
Of the Ford, he waits for her. He stands
With the posture of wheat in a field. The chew
From his bottom lip is tossed aside to the street
And he wipes his soiled thumb and forefinger
On his faded jeans. His handkerchief dabs
The leftover tobacco from his lips like a first kiss
Saved in a pocket. She now exits the store holding
A brown paper bag. He opens the passenger side door
For her, shuts it, and taps a knuckle to the glass.
The window falls like the warm evening light.

PAN-FRIED TOMATOES AT BREAKFAST

For Lila

My partner cuts tomatoes into wedges.
She says they're best pan-

Fried with olive oil, salt and pepper,
And cooked long enough to spread

On toasted sourdough. She insisted
On cooking by herself

This morning. She once told me
She didn't cook often but now

A pint glass brims with green
Onion on her kitchen counter—

This aroma lingers on her finger-
Tips. My partner says,

Try this, and I do. After she's done,
She hands me a plate

And sets the other in front of her-
Self and takes me

To where we are both consumed. She says,
Forget how hot they are, just eat.

TOMORROW,

For Jeff and Natalie

Because we'll find meaning in washing dishes.
Because the trees will fruit because we trust them to.
Because there is sometimes a line between
     where the ocean and the sky meet.
Because the forecast calls for rain.
Because to reach is enough.
Because a flood doesn't mean destruction.
Because some fires wisp into dust and looming
     beams of light.
Because the asters will hum if we listen.
Because, if we listen, the braided water hushes past.
Because we'll find in us a breathless room
     the way we stomached turning thirty.
Because bone-chill.
Because, when a flower wilts, we'll call it an extended hand.
Because the palm holds the weight of our memories.
Because of the fear of losing.
Because the distance we know and the distance
     we don't are the same thing.
Because we'll add salt and pepper to taste.
Because we'll call it a life together;
Because a life in which we know one breath
     doesn't always lead to another.
Because today, I've loved—I love—
How the glint off water and the reflection of sky makes
     suns of us both.

A PICTURE WINDOW. A HOUSE.

Flowers bought and left unplanted.
A life worth looking at
Beckoned toward this future—

*

Every spring, less and less sky:
Milkweed, cottonwood, and wild geranium.
So much shadow.

*

A life worth looking at is a touched life,
The shape of the world in a palm:
A fist. Jaw-clench.
A breath holding a mouth.

*

Eventually this life is only looked at.
The draw of a curtain:
Glittered ceilings that only feel like stars
Sighing into every room.

*

A hand reaching out in sleep. Then
You opened your eyes.
How fast I cannot really remember.

FLOWERS

I used to watch my mother cut flowers at the kitchen sink after she left my father. We lived in an apartment in the shape of an octagon.

I've put so many flowers—some vibrant, beautiful; some shallow with wilt—in the only glass vase I've owned since.

Was this some form of transfer?

*

I don't remember flowers before my mother left my father, but I do remember sitting on the kitchen counter in Saint Paul, Nebraska watching my mother cook.

*

Were there flowers after that apartment?

*

Here: hormonal bath.

*

Kneel as if to ready for prayer and open spit-mouth

Into the bald flowers bloating with insignificance,

Bloating with the fear of dying if they can't see

The sun dress their body as they die.

The purple eyes turning black:

How they carry

The worlds it took for those eyes to brighten.

Even the sun thought about Icarus slapping

Like blood-salad into the cloth-sea.

*

When I see purple flowers, I think of my father's corpse
Speaking to me:
How the ground opened enough for me
To fall and wake myself.
This went on for months.

*

The winter rain has lifted the fog slightly.

*

Recently, I felt the petals of a pink white amaryllis flower at the
Saturday morning Farmer's Market in Toledo, Ohio. Their heads
bowed, scanning their surroundings. Gently, my fingers rubbed
the petals and I remarked on how thick they were—how pretty the
red veined through the white. I thought of my mother and those
moments of transition. I thought of Lila beaming into mother-
hood. It was me who I left out of every equation, every decora-
tion, every breath of memory and I wanted to be in love with my
own life the way each flower I remembered has ever loved a room.

STILL LIFE

It's hard to know how solid the body
Until a hand exchanges its palm for another.

What I do know is that we reach into
Resilience much like we lean first

Into curtains of branch and leaf. Listen
To the crush of carpetweed

And bull thistle and shepherd's purse
Extend violent spears to sudden

The air still in them. That is, the wind bends
Through us. Even the trees carry the weight

Of extinction on their branches. All of this
Just to say: I feel full again.

IN A FIELD OF SOFT THUDS

You find a grasshopper pinned
In between the tines of the berry
Picker. When you remove it,
A brown liquid drips
From its mouth
As far from sweet
Today as it had ever been,
And you return
To winnowing the leaves
And stems from the buckets
Of foraged fruit. You sift through
Sweet fern, bastard toadflax,
And sand cherry to scrub yourself
Raw of the endless plumes
Of ash on your hands.
What you love takes shape
Inside your chest: a clattering
Like fresh budding leaves
That blossoms into mouth
But sometimes, you realize,
A prayer is just that, a prayer.
When splashing your exposed
Back from the well makes
Your cupped hands brim
With water, you drink as droplets
Slip past striking your boots
Echoing grasshopper.
And then this life was nothing
That surprised you.

NOTES

"Adorning the Table:": Ekphrasis of Victoria DuBourg's *Still Life with Flowers and Peaches*, oil on canvas, c. 1874.

"The Art of Hatching": After Kevin Young's "Hive."

"Carrion, or Something Like It": The poem takes inspiration from the FBI file "Animal Mutilation," part 1 of 5. p. 6, from 21 January 1975 on *The FBI: Federal Bureau of Investigation*, US Department of Justice at https://vault.fbi.gov/Animal%20Mutilation.

"First Snow, Under the Carillon": After Gabrielle Bates' "Sabbath."

"Pan-Fried Tomatoes at Breakfast": After Callista Buchen's "Bread."

"Thoughts on Exiting a Building": Ekphrasis of Fengyi Xu's *Untitled*, 8in. x 11in., Digital Photography, c. 2022.

ABOUT THE AUTHOR

Tyler Michael Jacobs is the author of *The Weight of Drought* (Stephen F. Austin State University Press) and *Building Brownville* (Stephen F. Austin State University Press). His words have appeared or are forthcoming in *Passages North, Variant Literature, Plainsongs, Pidgeonholes, Sierra Nevada Review,* and elsewhere. His poems have also been featured on Nebraska Public Media's *Friday LIVE.* He received his MFA from Bowling Green State University.

www.ingramcontent.com/pod-product-compliance
Lightning Source LLC
Jackson TN
JSHW080211070525
83923JS00007B/26

* 9 7 8 1 6 2 2 8 8 2 8 6 1 *